THIS LAST TIME WILL BE THE FIRST

THIS LAST TIME WILL BE THE FIRST

Jeff Alessandrelli

Burnside Review Press   Portland, Oregon

This Last Time Will Be The First
© 2014 Jeff Alessandrelli

Cover Image: Stan VanDerBeek, "Untitled (Breathdeath)," 1963
Collage and ink on board
Courtesy of the Estate of Stan VanDerBeek

Cover Design: Regina Godfrey
Layout: Shira Richman

Thank you to Literary Arts, whose publishing fellowship
contributed to the making of this book.

Printed in the U.S.A.
First Edition, 2014
ISBN: 978-0-9895611-2-9

Burnside Review Press
Portland, Oregon
www.burnsidereview.org

Burnside Review Press titles are available for purchase from the
publisher and Small Press Distribution (www.spdbooks.org).

I. PEOPLE ARE PLACES ARE PLACES ARE PEOPLE

I.

PEOPLE ARE PLACES ARE PLACES ARE PEOPLE

Dear Sir,—

I am in a Madhouse & quite forget your Name or who you are. You must excuse me for I have nothing to communicate or tell you of & why I am shut up I don't know I have nothing to say so I conclude

Yours respectfully
John Clare

One morning—I'm not sure why, maybe some type of lack or definition or half-tawdry want—I woke up, saw my neighbor's bike lying in his driveway and just beat the shit out of it, just pummeled and crumpled and wracked and irrevocably dismantled it until what it was couldn't even be called "bike" anymore; it was something else entirely. Then I went to work. When I got home that night my neighbor's driveway was empty, his garage door closed. The bike was gone, all its recognizable parts absent, vanished, shaped into new and heretofore incalculable realities.

UNDERSTANDING MINA LOY (EVERYTHING, EVERYTHING,
EVERYTHING)

I will refrain from discussing
the role of the lover.

Always burn the sheets
after you fuck in them.

Every orphanage is a womb

> stretched
> towards a bursting point.

Birth is sheathes and sheathes

> of paperwork, some signatures
> and the hopeful solemnity of a handclasp

while walking into a fluorescent-filled room.

> Oliver Twist was a C-section
> that snuck away

and kept on running.

> He eventually learned how to steal,
> learned how to shape the idea of a mother

out of a hot meal cooked

> over a low fire,
> the starlight over his shoulders

so blindingly blindingly bright.

> I'm nothing special.
> I always touch the straw to my lips.

A person is considered crazy if

they only have one story to tell.
And every orphan has at least two.

Cloud fields change into furniture
furniture metamorphizes into fields
an emphasis falls on reality.

And I was envious,
am envious.

It is only
the imagination
that can resist
the imagination,

it is only the imagination
that can withstand,
uphold, subvert
and resist

the imagination.

The paper arrives
        electronic,
our dog

only fetches
        balls and sticks.
Which is symptomatic

of a fallen culture,
        one that no longer understands
the importance

of a properly rigid cultivation
        says an old man
sitting in a dirty lawn chair

directly in the middle
        of our dying front lawn.
He is an old man

wearing
        nothing but
 an oversized fur shawl

and an abandoned bird's nest
        as a hat.
Wild hairs blossom

on the hills and valleys
        of his thighs and chest.
He doesn't blink.

The dog doesn't bark.
        Our computer is folded
into itself and fully

charged.
        Father, life isn't
necessary, but living

happily is?
        How will one ever learn
these years are a test?

"WE ARE TOLD, FOR EXAMPLE, THAT RALPH WALDO
EMERSON, WHILE HE DISAPPROVED OF LAUGHTER, DID
OCCASIONALLY ALLOW HIMSELF TO SMILE, BUT HE DID SO
ONLY WITH HIS EYES CLOSED."—JULIAN HAWTHORNE

A fleetingly glimpsed smile
is a homesickness

for the comfort
of what in all

likelihood
should have remained

hidden from view

in the first place.
Then always remember

not to point and laugh
at my well-spruced forest

of back hair
when I'm swimming

at the beach.
O you lonely anthologists

of still born moments

and awkward silences,
of nervous blinking,

clammy hands,
greasy handshakes,

close, for once, your eyes.

There is a light
so bright there

that it can oftentimes
be difficult to see.

But stroll with me
for a while now

anyway. I have
freshly baked blueberry

muffins that we can eat,
then turn into so

many crumbs
at our feet.

I know a bawdy

yet ultimately harmless
joke that we can chuckle

over before one
of us starts to

uncontrollably spit,
ceaselessly choke.

Close your eyes.
No one, nothing is smiling or waiting.

"AND JUST AS HE HAD ALREADY LOST HIS SKEPTICISM, SO
NOW HE BEGAN GRADUALLY TO LOSE HIS SELF-CONTROL
AND THE REST OF HIS GOOD SENSE ALSO."—JAROSLAV
HAŠEK

Once I denied myself nothing
because I knew, later, I would be shameful
of everything my diet guru tells me.
Her eyes are of a blind infant's only blue,
her posture that of a smoke signal's
corkscrewed yet relentless ascent.
The full name of my diet guru's eleven-year-old son
is Christopher Maximilien Douglas Schmidt,
she's informed me on several occasions.
The first step is realizing
that by its very existence
the strawberries and cream parfait
is smarter than you. A world to refuse
everywhere you look. Some music
to guide you in and out of each.
Austria got Hungary and fried Turkey
in Greece she tells me by way of admonishment.
People die every day and are reborn
just as quickly. People grow into their bodies
and can grow right back out.
My diet guru with the flat blue eyes
and posture tells me that when
she was a child in elementary school
she was unpopular, always the last
to get a chance on the swing set,
always having to do all the hard work
herself. *Behind me there was nothing*
but the ghost of a push she says.
I am here, I am slowly cinderelling myself
into focus and position. Fitful, listless,
all of the music is coming around.

"IF YOU LIVE LONG ENOUGH, YOU'LL SEE THAT EVERY
VICTORY TURNS INTO A DEFEAT."—SIMONE DE BEAUVOIR

The frame extends   well-beyond
its picture, the same strange way

there are supposedly only three fruits
native to North America—

the cranberry, the blueberry and the Concord grape—
and yet North America

imports more types and varieties of fruit
than any other country in the world.

According to Simone de Beauvoir
an adult is nothing but a child

blown up by age, someone
who doesn't actually know

how young he or she is
but verily verily knows

how old he or she isn't.
Today it is the fourth

day of the first week
of the new year

and steadily blown up by age
I am squinting into the faint radiance

of the sun, its light
trying to shine

through the still born ribs
of the ever-encompassing clouds.

Remembering
that you used

to have someone to miss:
a kind of New Year's resolution.

I'm still not going to teach
your boyfriend

how to dance with you,
not going to teach

at all.
Music blasting out car windows

to the left and right of me,
it's not it's not it's not

the radios
that sing.

When it came to Alcibiades' studies, he was fairly obedi-
ent to most of his teachers, but refused to learn the flute,
which he regarded as an ignoble accomplishment and quite
unsuitable for a free citizen. He argued that to use a plec-
trum and play the lyre does not disfigure a gentleman's
bearing or appearance, but once a man starts blowing into
a flute, his own friends can scarcely recognize his features.
Besides, the lyre accompanies and creates a harmony for
the words or the song of its performer, but the flute seals
and barricades his mouth and deprives him both of voice
and of speech. *Leave the flute to the sons of Thebes*, he conclud-
ed, *for they have no idea of conversation. We Athenians, as our fathers
say, have Athena for our foundress and Apollo for our patron, one of whom
threw away the flute in disgust, while the other stripped the skin off the man
who played it!*[1] In this way, half in jest and half in earnest, he
not only avoided learning the instrument himself, but in-
duced the other boys to do the same. The word soon went
round that Alcibiades detested flute-playing and made fun
of everybody who learned it, and with good reason, too.
In consequence the flute disappeared from the number of
so-called liberal accomplishments and came to be utterly
despised.

[1] Athena is said to have thrown away the flute on seeing the unflattering
effect on her features mirrored in a spring. Apollo defeated Marsyas in
a musical contest and flayed him alive.

I was at a rock
and roll performance—
a show!—
and right
before
the last song
the lead singer
noticed
one of his Chuck Taylor's
was untied.
He noticed

one of his sneakers
was untied
and then he bent
down and untied
the other sneaker.
Displayed himself
to us.
All of us
in the crowd cheered
wildly.
And then they
played their last
song, their biggest
smash hit.

Bad pop songs make my throat hurt
in the same way that old soul songs—
Sam Cooke and Wilson Pickett
simultaneously lamenting and exalting
with the very same note—
remind me that I don't have a soul,
that no one has a soul.
Fate can spell hate backwards,
can spell attenuating, can spell
bliss. Forever
the smartest dumb guy in the room,
of his heroin abuse
Lenny Bruce said
I'll die young, but it's like
kissing God.
He once lost his voice
singing at the wedding
of a twice-removed cousin of his,
one that he hardly even knew.
How he wept and cried at the ceremony.
Sometimes I wake up
in the morning
and install the flowers wrong
and later they're still shining
and resonating
in the sun anyway.
Sometimes I read
the approaching landscape
wrong, the way I
once did as a child.
Bone by tremulous bone

I advance myself
into the world.
With the radio,
in the shower,
I often can't stop
singing and singing.
On the best of days
it's enough.

"STRANGE VICTORY! STRANGE VICTORY! STRANGE VICTORY!
STRANGE DEFEAT."—DAVID BERMAN

With the speared nub
of his unopened umbrella,

the man stabs
at the snake's taut stalk

of a body.
Invisible hands,

invisible arms, invisible feet,
the snake rises up

straight in response.
Between the trees

late-morning wads
of sunshine douse

both man and snake in light.
The umbrella's handle

is dark brown, custom-made.
O how the abandoned

abandon
the abandoned

abandon the abandoned.

The snake is very real
and very alert.

Watch.

When the 20th century French avant-garde composer Erik Satie died no one had been in his apartment in 27 years, and when his brother and the four chosen friends did eventually enter inside they discovered a lifetime still festering: in one corner of the room four plucked and gutted pianos, two back to back, two stacked on top of the other two and in every other corner countless particles of dirt and dust. They found a great trove of Satie's personal drawings and doodles, many of intricately designed medieval buildings; *castles in lead*. And numerous piano compositions, some previously unknown, some thought to be lost forever, among them Satie's *Vexations* (which it was soon discovered took 18+ hours to play) and new variations on his already famous *Gnossienne* and "furniture music" pieces, ones that anticipated both ambient and conceptual music. They found an assortment of love letters, never sent, addressed to the artist Suzanne Valadon, the sole woman Satie is known to have slept with. And more doodles and drawings, more unopened, unsent letters. They found seven velvet suits and too many cobwebs to count. They found upwards of 100 umbrellas, dozens of them still encased in wrapping, obviously never used. All his life Erik Satie was known to hate sunshine, preferring instead the rain, preferring instead every type of inclement weather. Up and down the streets he walked, composing in his head so many haunting and beautiful songs impossible to hum, impossible to sing, impossible to whistle. The rain arrived in chunks and layers all around him and Erik Satie never looked up, never acknowledged the rain's presence. His shoes got wet. And staring at his feet, Erik Satie listened to what was already coming next. He did shiver.

Gertrude Stein once opened an umbrella indoors, that much is clear. You can read about it in the "Objects" section of *Tender Buttons*, under "An Umbrella":

Coloring high means that the strange reason is in front not more in front behind. Not more in front in peace of the dot.

She never forgot that moment, her errant fingers, the umbrella extending itself outwards of its own accord, her instantaneous sorrow, her great lamentation. For the rest of Gertrude Stein's life she lived in the swift certitude of that umbrella's unfolding.

Gertrude Stein was not a superstitious woman. No. But when she walked the Parisian streets

afterwards

in the rain

Gertrude Stein insisted Alice hold an umbrella upside down,

just in front,   high above her head.

Alice caught a lot of rain in it.

If the size of the raindrop, its splash,
        is affected by the color of your eyes,

if the setting sun, its endless game of hide and seek,
        is a fine way to ruin your supper,

if your nipples are the cold unseeing
        eyes of your breasts,

if in your city starlight does not exist
        but for the streetlamps' weary weary hum,

if you often choose to wash your hands with fire,
        to dry them with bark and dusky chalk,

if the body is a type of coffin,
        the mind a half-futile release,

if I am able to forgive what I cannot forget
        about what you once desired
to say and create,

then each and every moment here
        on earth is a place you have never been
until you arrive into it.

I am writing Paradise.

(I am not *trying* to write it.)

I am writing Paradise.

Outside my window

the wind hears nothing

but its own rustle.

Pink and green and day-glo red

bullets pass by and pass on.

In Paradise every stone is a mirror,

one that presents a most imperfect reflection.

In Paradise thy vanity scatters.

In Paradise the beauty of your face

is only what you can feel

with your hands.

Paradise is the wind sailing

into the trees, trees

reacting to the wind.

We were a pair of lonely sexual markets, each hinging on
the social development of our various foreign outputs. Ev-
erything for me was a dilemma—imports and exports, the
rational anti-rationalization towards the inherency of free
will and trade. You had the opposite problem: Incoming
and outgoing, your goods had been accepted so easily for
so often and so long that they were of little worth to you or
anyone else. We came together like two gigantic icebergs
mired in a child's empty wading pool. Nothing else to lean
against, nothing else to touch. *It's a joy selling quality products
again to someone that actually appreciates them* you said with a smile.
*My how money has the power to change the world to the point where now
I'm finally able to see it* I lovingly replied. So much is paradise,
marketwise and fleeting. And the problems that never start
never stop. Then behind every window another potential
partner or secret admirer, everywhere in sight a more al-
luring sale or possible trade.

Elsie Stevens was not ass-ugly,
as is sometimes thought.
Her hazelnut eyes were
beautiful, her hair
a dark dark brown.

Unlike her Harvard-educated husband Wallace,
she barely passed the sixth grade
and had no interest
in continuing
her schooling further.

Great laborious crumbs
of oily skin
put her husband's face
prominently in place
but with Elsie
you were sometimes liable

to barely see her
even as you stared.

Unlike her failure of a husband—
his mind betraying himself
to itself—
Elsie suffered
no wanton perversity
of the imagination.

She loved flowers.
She tolerated funerals.
She laughed and laughed
and laughed

at even funnier jokes.

A brain secretes thought as a liver secretes bile. Accidents aren't the same thing as mistakes, but your ideas regarding the difference between the two just might be. From close range the French entomologist Jean-Henri Fabre once fired a cannon at a tree full of relentlessly chirping cicadas and not a note of their song was altered, not a beat missed. They were entirely undisturbed. This proves not that cicadas are deaf; it merely proves that cicadas are not thinking while searching—singing—for a mate, and certainly not about cannon blasts. The massed brain secretes each and every thought as the liver secretes vacuous, guileful, greenish-orange bile. Even when absent, out of view, bile itself is a kind of thought; the liver, however, decidedly not. A white semicircle stapled to a piece of black construction paper and taped on the ceiling we painted a watery dull yellow, lots of unattributable wings floating around, I've been working on my idea for a map of the entire universe. In love with its own faultiness, it's a work in progress, plangent thoughts inside plangent thought.

During his lifetime pursuit as a professional daredevil Evel Knievel broke 433 bones, a Guinness World Record.

Over 100 countries grow shrimp, which is more than grow corn or wheat.

Sixty million people were killed during World War II. Only fifteen million people were killed during World War I.

One day I want to meet someone named Allison Wonderlund.

The Grecian god Tantalus was kicked out of Olympus for, among other things, cannibalism, human sacrifice and infanticide. He was banished to Tartarus, the deepest, netherest region of the Underworld. He endlessly suffered, but always with hope of redemption. With a feverish expectancy. From Tantalus the verb *to tantalize* is derived.

The first Kentucky Fried Chicken opened in Utah.

There are 4,058,347 million miles of road in the United States. 91% are paved.

Most of the time I like the pink candies best, better than the red ones, better than the green ones, better than yellow.

"Everything changed when Morgan the Magician arrived."

A standard 12 ounce slice of prime rib has 1165 calories,

offering its consumer 225% of the Food and Drug Administration's suggested fat intake for the day.

In 1906 Alois Alzheimer identified the first published case of presenile dementia (later to become known as Alzheimer's disease) in the person of Auguste Deter. In Alzheimer's examination of Deter, the following conversation between doctor and patient took place:

"What is your name?"
"Auguste."
"Family name?"
"Auguste."
"What is your husband's name?" —she hesitates, finally answers:
"I believe... Auguste."
"Your husband?"
"Oh, so!"
"How old are you?"
"Fifty-one."
"Where do you live?"
"Oh, you have been to our place."
"Are you married?"
"Oh, I am so confused."
"Where are you right now?"
"Here and everywhere, here and now, you must not think badly of me."
"Where are you at the moment?"
"This is where I will live."
"Where is your bed?"
"Where should it be?"

And this one, taken from Alzheimer's transcribed notes:

Around midday, Frau Auguste D. ate pork and cauliflower—

"What are you eating?"
"Spinach." (She was chewing meat.)

"What are you eating now?"
"First I eat potatoes and then horseradish."
"Write a '5'."
She writes: "A woman"
"Write an '8'."
She writes: "Auguste" (While she is writing she again says, "It's like I have lost myself.")

Fifteen million people, sixty million people.

433 broken bones. 1165 calories and 225%.

Tantalus is waiting expectantly. He knows and knows he will be saved.

"Everything changed when Morgan the Magician arrived."

The pink pink candies.

Alois Alzheimer died at the age of 51, of heart failure. Auguste Deter died at the age of 56, of what by the time of her death had already become known as Alzheimer's disease.

The hard bright sweet sticky pink candies.

"Everything changed when Morgan the Magician arrived."

4,058,347 miles. 4,058,347 million miles.

It's like I have lost myself again.

In memoriam Lewis Wright

Glazed clean
little dollops

of consciousness.

Waiting for
what's always just

about to happen
next, we sit

here and the glittery
stars answer

only to the sun

answer only
to the stars.

To the splitting
floridity of the darkness

and to the twinkly stars.

Even looking half-amassed
like that your long

perennial selves

are sure worth knowing
and smooching

and seeming.

How an outstretched hand
can simultaneously appear as a fist.

Can act like one.

And then—not lost,

not roaming, ever-mendacious,
brawling light

of the mind, seared—

what we miss   instead

The shadow puppets of our youth:
now two bulbous, knuckle-happy fists
reflecting on a stranger's chalk white wall.

Still, I love nights like this,
my face soggily loose
leaf notebooking into itself,

each wrinkle leaving
behind no more
than a riddle's traceable clues.

What have I seen,
now see? There were
times before
I look now

Creeley once mumbled to himself,
thinking about ice cream
and his misspent and idealized youth.

In the dark, we can cleanly imagine as much.
To see where I was going at night
I used to sleep with the lights on.

You were always true.

I have found the secret
Of loving you

Always for the first time
Breton insisted, his wife's bangs

veiling her dark eyes.
A somnambulist, Breton believed love

was nothing if not the answer
to a series of unposed questions

posed by an invisible someone else
as irrefutable facts.

The night is an expensive toy
no one can read the instructions to.

The result of a bad translation perhaps,
one mumbled and scattered, without end.

This afternoon—a very beautiful one,
grass & clouds & trees—

I wandered the hills aimlessly,
in search of nothing.

I smelled lilac I think. Jasmine.
And: André Breton is a liar.

With foul, horribly foul breath.

God counts the darkness
while we sleep.
Burrowing inside the dark
sky of His mind.
And wonders about His duty
to the blind, deaf
and faithful.

God wants
as the world
wants.

The wicked are estranged from the womb.
Those who speak lies go astray from birth.

Counting the darkness,
God wants
and wants
as the world.

Remarkable hobbyist,

God looks at us
the same way
we look at
an old receipt.

Remembering is Hell
where it came from.

"I SING JUST TO KNOW I'M ALIVE."—NINA SIMONE

Like a hanged man

whose rope has stretched taut

the sun sets in the mountains

with a quickness.

The lungs and ribs of every cloud

are newly born and transparent.

You can see the stars!

Counting the darkness is impossible, verily impossible!

Back in town if your boss thinks you're guilty of something

you're guilty of something,

but not out here, not tonight.

In the mountains

and when the sun goes down

and the thicked marble slab of the dark.

Your cheeks, your eyelashes, are anti-heirs

to a thousand municipal ordinances here.

The ruddy dirt, the announced silence.

The unannounced silence.

You can see the stars tonight!

Shining and bright!

II.

JEFFREY ROBERTS' DREAMCOATS

I is another.

—Arthur Rimbaud

He believes
that even if
his parents had never
been born,
his grandparents never
having met
at the dance
or dinner party
or lake house retreat,
he nevertheless

still would have.
It takes mere seconds
to make a man.
He claims
to have found
the Fountain of Youth
using Google Maps.
Where is Florida?
Brussels?

A dream-thinned child.

A wounded animal
that doesn't yet realize
he's lost
both sight and scent
of the pack up ahead.

His silly billy-goat-beard
cleanly divorcing his face
from his face.

His brown eyes,
his gangly limbs.

His teeth and ratty brown sneakers.

My *most* imaginary friend.

At the job interview I am dead already, a lone wolf fleeing in a direct line across a great expanse of newly fallen snow, the guttural sounds of my hunters behind me. Across that expanse I leave every trace of my death in the unremitting whiteness. I am wearing a navy blue sports jacket and a navy blue tie made with elements of corrugated lead and iron. I mumble. I perspire, the sense of sensation at the nape of my neck, at the base of my collar, faulty and irreparable. At the interview's end I shake characteristically weighted hands and bike home in the dusk, in the impending dark, thinking about how Alexander the Great slept with a copy of *The Iliad* under his pillow because he wished to attain the same eternal glory that Odysseus and Achilles and Hector had attained. I lost that little black portable carrier clip thing for my cell phone. I haven't lost the actual phone—at least not yet—but when someone calls, anyway, I prefer to text. Pointing it out is banal and stupid, I know, but everyone breathes the same invisibilities in the air. Blood's red. Knock knock. Who's there? *There is no Other of the Other and anyone who claims to take up this place is an imposter*, Jacques Lacan is always telling me in a haughty French accent. Tonight I am that imposter, biking home alone in the dark. I have a pet turtle named Spike. He never responds when I call him. He never answers. Sometimes I call him Ike.

In order to get himself to finish his dissertation he once shaved half his head, leaving the other half long, still flirting with his shoulders. It was so that he could *focus*, would be forced to work and work, would be too embarrassed to leave the house. Now, years later, he has two jobs, maybe three, sometimes three. Sometimes two.

This afternoon, today, right now, he is standing in the middle of a greeny clearing, the sun covering him in gold. His shadow stains the surrounding landscape a wisp of black. He never learned how to whistle. One day he hopes to learn.

His baggy pants, his backwards hat, his ballooned-out shirt, dirty blue bandanna, shoes two sizes too big for his narrow feet—the fact that he's ugly on purpose makes him more of a sexpot. Dressing in clothes that don't fit properly is one way to refuse the future. There are several others.

He is standing in the middle of a greeny clearing, right now, today, blankly regarding oak and apple country. Birds are whistling from branches. Dusk arrives easy.

I was born with two wings,
one of them broken.

By the end of our lives
our posture blames us
for everything, everything.

Up the lonely slices
of the narrow streets
we walk.

Memory reminds me of a stupendous fire spreading and
spreading and spreading and then suddenly ceasing, ex-
tinguished.

Orgasms remind me of stupendous fires spreading and
spreading and spreading and then suddenly ceasing, ex-
tinguished.

From some basement
on a hill,
we all die equally.

Long is life and beautiful.

III.

IT IS ESPECIALLY DANGEROUS TO BE CONSCIOUS OF ONESELF

There was a man who was born in Yen but grew up in Ch'u, and in old age returned to his native country. While he was passing through the state of Chin his companions played a joke on him. They pointed out a city and told him: "This is the capital of Yen." He composed himself and looked solemn. Inside the city they pointed out a shrine: "This is the shrine of your quarter." He breathed a deep sigh. They pointed out a hut: "This was your father's cottage." His tears welled up. They pointed out a mound: "This is your father's tomb." He could not help weeping aloud. His companions roared with laughter: "We were teasing you. You are still only in Chin." The man was very embarrassed. When he reached Yen, and really saw the capital of Yen and the shrine of his quarter, really saw his father's cottage and tomb, he did not feel it so deeply.

—**From** *The Book of Lieh-tz'u*

According to the fancy new guidebook I bought, you don't go crazy all by yourself. Out of some freshly sealed envelope of darkness, every morning we have to invent the sun in order to see it, have to invent the sky's cherry-blue backdrop in order to witness the sun's milky light. Eventually there comes a point, though, when our inventions fail us: patentless, faulty, we wake up in some vaguely familiar pitch black. Yesterday was different we think, without entirely understanding how or why. But now it is the first day of spring and—reverent—we take the time to remember. Today is the first day of spring. Half-weighted flashlights aimed and ready, we ceaselessly pray that we will never ever have less.

Puppies are born deaf, blind and basically helpless,
    Not even opening their eyes until they are two weeks old.

      To see a world in a grain of sand Blake said,
        But which—one containing only the lumbersome joggers

That I speed past on my way to work every morning,
    Or world where no matter how many times I roll down my window

      Up and down, over and over, they still don't care
        To notice my huge fucking biceps?

In the trickle-quick world down at the beach the water's lapping
    Lapping tongues desire to lap up every single grain for themselves.

      And today and today and every other day, the shore is restless,
        Some of the dogs on the beach barking,

Some panting, some running, sleeping,
    Some of the dogs are listening,

      Standing very very still, eyes wide.

(MOTHER)

My mother is my latest idea, only in yellow
this time, furtive hints of mauve and hot pink.
And I choose to believe that as a child
someone at the county fair told my mother
that the bright stars above her were really fireworks

that neglecting to burst, neglecting to fall,
were left hanging up in the sky, stuck,
gradually losing their greens, reds and blues. Luster.
You celebrate the same old celebrations
night after night after night after night

I choose to believe my mother was told.
My grandmother was a horse
that could not talk but loved to listen.
How she galloped down every road available to her,
uncontrollably sneezing with her entire face.

(FATHER)

I grew up in a house

made out of smoke
and old mental carvings.

Father disrobed in it
the way a man stranded for decades

on a deserted island

might disrobe.
Was a superbly prolific eater, father.

Mother loved life and to work.

Today I live in a house
feeling I'm constantly dreaming

what I might once have been

busy being.

It chafes,
clutter's reverberation

with sound.

Poems are not about
the difference between

what you know

and what you choose to reveal.

Poems are about houses.

(CRUSTS)

Eating the crusts
of yesterday, refusing
them, hungering
for more. Landslides
and landslides of poetry.
Lava spills. I am
tardy with myself
in the way
you no doubt feel
about me. Blinking
an ill-advised act
of meditation.
Policy actualizes
nothing.
Fathers make nothing

happen. Elegantly
meandering tavern stories
make nothing happen.
In the simulation, the
beautifully white bunnies
hopping through the
weedy, grassy, green
and dirt-spurned field
make nothing happen.
Yesterday's crusts. Land-
slides and landslides.
Fevers. Lava spills
ordered and over.
Mere policy. Or Policy.
Poetry is.

(ZOMBIES)

Drunken sailors at a homecoming's
weekend-long happy hour,

my teeth clink and clink together.

Sweat nevertheless
inexplicably

grumbles out of me.

I do not believe in zombies.
I do not believe that

from the inside
my mind is being eaten
alive

by the deadgod repellant

of my own every thought.

I do not do not believe that.

I can hear clouds
merging and passing above me.

If I could I would
dream a little dream,

one of the brazen calmness
of a waterfall's gaping crotch.

The sun is a byproduct
of an infinitude of marigolds
and pure supple honey, here.

It's easy to find
the lost city of Atlantis
in every dog's water bowl, here.

Every step before, behind and ahead
lands in a mousetrap or an empty shark
tank held up at the corners

by a series of inexacting secrets,
here. Here

we press snowflakes into the static
pages of a book the same way
others press flowers

and those snowflakes stay
perfectly intact, indelible, true.
We muscle our way in

with our hearts, here.
We're as beautiful as we wish
to desire to be,

once upon a time,
here, here, here,
here, here.

(MIRAGE)

A low, ponderous country
where the clouds are a series of disparate thoughts
and the rain they insist on reasoning with
a celebration of their hectic musings.
The men are watering the streets anyways.
Luminous, just-fresh, the concrete sparkles;
gum stains and spit stains and every veritable crack.
Do they still call mirrors looking glasses anymore?
Those type of tempered thoughts.
Yo I'm lazy but I'm crazy too
You never know what I definitely might do
threatens the radio, mass-eyed and alert.
Up ahead the mirage is steady and punctual.
We're waiting for a war to begin
or a delectable sweet to eat after lunch.

Realizing that breaking every finite bone

    in his readily measurable body

        is a kind of insouciant attitude,

an elaborately attentive, half-pliant pose,

    in midair he teaches himself

        the idea of home, its always expected

sensation, marked and rendered

    comfort, calm. Wobbled knots

        of air but paused,

then the fall,

    his still-definitive conclusion.

(JACKS)

A group of children playing jacks.
And the balls they bounce as—
in motion with nothing beyond want of the game,
its absolute measure—
they grab for onesie, twosie,
three, are bright and shiny.

And the sound of their hands clapping
dissolves quickly into the texture of the air.

And here in this country,
does the land grow or our stubby legs running blindly
    after it?

Out in front the clouds are half-pale scabs
on the ceaseless patina of the sky.

Without realizing it they are thinking about whispering to
    us
so much of what they have already shouted.
It's raining up ahead. Then it's pouring, simply pouring.

(LIMBS)

The audible shape
        of a billowing scream,

                avalanche that was born milk-white
and died dark dark red.

        The sun shining;
                the resort's holiday weekend package.

Too many birds staring
        from the newly understood limbs

                of an upstanding tree.

(SKY)

The sky
isn't
butcher knife
bloody red
today,
doesn't look
like a tender wound
that's been a-lifetime
a-festering.

We look
older
than we feel
and
younger
than we are.

Today,
it's a gift,

the same way
you're forever
a child
in every antique store.

The vase is glass,
the china crystal,
the butter

silks and sweats
right off
of your hands.

(MOON)

The full moon
is a snowball

packed tight,

constantly trailing
after,
endlessly hoping
to hit,

the earth's
shrouded, shivering
face.

The sun
knows no future
and no past

but itself,

its warmth
and its light.

Mocks
us.

The stars
are not satellites

glued

to the flimsy
2D surface
of the sky.

They are not
the viscous and frozen
remnants
of some ancient god's
hocked up
and out
phlegm,

are not
so many shining sterling

umbrellas

opened up
against
the darkness

of the night.

The stars are dead,

that's all.

All of the stars

are just dead.

(TOMORROW)

And supposing tomorrow we are finally rich
against the morning, the streets
scrubbed clean of concrete, asphalt and tar,
property lines extended skyward,
limbs no longer
indebted to our bodies
but splayed further, distant,
not a glass or plastic jar in sight
but still an abundance of peanut butter,
guilt-free boysenberry jam,
and then believing all this only
to consider
what the percentage is
in closing your eyes
and turning around,
desperately looking back.

(SHARKS)

The truth of the brittle, infirm spider
lies in the fly

caught in a mesh of web
the spider can no longer reach.

Do you believe in reincarnation?
I hope to be creatively satisfied

in the same manner as the windmill
and jetstream.

When I grow up. It's hot all over.
How the sun makes me sing.

All morning long I've been walking
the plank and still haven't hit

water. Don't let me forget
to feed the sharks.

They have a tendency
to unfairly react

to things like that.
I'll miss you.

Once upon a time.

It is especially dangerous to be conscious of oneself.

You lose it if you talk about it.

It is especially dangerous

to be conscious of oneself.

IV.

YOU CAN'T DISCOVER THE LOST TREASURE IF THE SHIP
DIDN'T SINK

The world is perfect

and that's the problem.

You can't discover

the lost treasure

if the ship didn't sink.

This last time

will be the first.

ACKNOWLEDGEMENTS

Some of these poems, often in different forms, previously appeared in *Gulf Coast*; *Octopus*; *DIAGRAM*; *Forklift, Ohio*; *Handsome*; *CutBank*; *U City Review*; *Denver Quarterly*; *Redivider*; *Nashville Review*; *Anti–*; *Everyday Genius*; *Whiskey Island*; *Hunger Mountain*; *South Dakota Review*; *Juked*; *Salt Hill*; *751 Magazine*; *diode*; *Timber*; and the chapbooks *Don't Let Me Forget To Feed The Sharks* (Poor Claudia, 2012) and *People Are Places Are Places Are People* (Imaginary Friend Press, 2013). My gratitude to the editors of each of those publications.

For their (conscious and unconscious) help, guidance and instruction during the writing and assembling of these poems I am indebted to the following people and animals: Joshua Ware, Trey Moody, Bret Shepard, John Chávez, Carrie Walker, Ian Huebert, Grace Bauer, Seanna Sumalee Oakley, Stephen Behrendt, Kwame Dawes, Zachary Schomburg, Michele Glazer, John Gallaher, Matthew Rohrer, Emily Pettit, Bill Knott, Sid Miller, Regina Godfrey, Dan Kaplan, Bill Bogart, Jenny Alessandrelli, Bob Alessandrelli, Mary Alessandrelli and Beckett Long Snout.

Also—Vietnamese salad rolls and hot bubble baths. Caramel. Thank you.

Jeff Alessandrelli is the author of the little book *Erik Satie Watusies His Way Into Sound* (Ravenna Press, 2011) and three chapbooks, including *Don't Let Me Forget To Feed The Sharks* (Poor Claudia, 2012). His work has appeared in *Denver Quarterly, Pleiades, DIAGRAM, Redivider, Salt Hill, Western Humanities Review, Gulf Coast* and *Boston Review,* among others. The name of his dog is Beckett Long Snout.

D1407924